BOOK ANALYSIS

Written by Flore Beaugendre
Translated by Rebecca Neal

Perceval, or, The Story of the Grail

BY CHRÉTIEN DE TROYES

Bright
≡Summaries.com

CHRÉTIEN DE TROYES	**1**
French poet	
PERCEVAL, OR, THE STORY OF THE GRAIL	**2**
One of the best examples of the courtly novel	
SUMMARY	**3**
Chrétien de Troyes' novel	
The continuations	
CHARACTER STUDY	**9**
Perceval	
Gawain	
ANALYSIS	**12**
A "novel"	
A coming-of-age novel	
Chivalry	
A complex structure	
FURTHER REFLECTION	**19**
Some questions to think about…	
FURTHER READING	**21**

CHRÉTIEN DE TROYES

FRENCH POET

- **Born around 1135.**
- **Died around 1183.**
- **Notable works**:
    - *Erec and Enide* (around 1170), novel
    - *Yvain, the Knight of the Lion* (around 1177), novel
    - *Lancelot, or, The Knight of the Cart* (around 1177-1181), novel

Chrétien de Troyes was born in around 1135 and died in around 1183. His name suggests that he was from the town of Troyes. We know very little about him, other than the small amount of information that can be gleaned from his writing. For example, we can suppose that he was a clerk and regular visitor to the court of Champagne, then the court of Philip of Alsace, Count of Flanders (1143-1191).

Chrétien de Troyes is a key figure of medieval literature, and is considered to be the first known author of chivalric romances. He wrote seven books in this genre, six of which are set in the Arthurian era. He wrote his most famous novels, *Yvain, the Knight of the Lion* and *Perceval, or, The Story of the Grail*, towards the end of his life.

PERCEVAL, OR, THE STORY OF THE GRAIL

ONE OF THE BEST EXAMPLES OF THE COURTLY NOVEL

- **Genre:** novel
- **Reference edition:** De Troyes, C. (2011) *Perceval, or, The Story of the Grail*. Trans. Cline, R.H. Athens, Georgia: University of Georgia Press.
- **1st edition:** 12th century
- **Themes:** coming of age, chivalry, exploits, Round Table

Perceval, or, The Story of the Grail was probably written in around 1181 and was left unfinished when its author died. It is dedicated to Chrétien de Troyes' patron, Philip of Alsace, Count of Flanders. The novel tells the story of Perceval, a young man who starts out naïve and ignorant but goes on to become a respected knight. The author alternates between his adventures and those of Gawain.

As the work was left unfinished, other authors wanted to write continuations to the adventures of Perceval and Gawain. Many later writers took up the story and made a variety of additions. With *Perceval, or, The Story of the Grail*, Chrétien was responsible for the spread of the Arthurian legend and the Matter of Britain.

SUMMARY

CHRÉTIEN DE TROYES' NOVEL

Perceval's adventures

Chrétien dedicates his book to his patron, Philip of Alsace, Count of Flanders, who he praises.

After meeting some knights for the first time, Perceval decides to go to King Arthur to be dubbed. His mother gives him three pieces of advice: serve ladies, seek the company of gentlemen, and pray. She then collapses as if dead.

On his way, the young man from Wales comes across a sleeping girl in a tent. He kisses her and steals her ring. The girl is in the depths of despair as her lover may become angry with her.

Perceval arrives at King Arthur's court and asks him to dub him, but the king puts it off until later. The young man then leaves to demand the clothes of the Red Knight, an enemy of the king, and manages to take his armour.

The young man meets the gentleman Gornemant of Gohort, who makes him a knight. Gornemant introduces him to his rank and gives him valuable advice, such as to avoid talking too much: "The wise man's saying's always been that 'Too much talking is a sin'" (p. 48).

Perceval arrives at the castle of Belrepeire, home to Blancheflor, which is under siege by King Clamadeu. The young man offers to take on the seneschal and the king himself in return for the beautiful lady's love. He emerges victorious.

Perceval leaves to find his mother again. He is given food and shelter by the Fisher King, who offers him an extraordinary sword. He witnesses the mysterious ceremony of the passage of the grail and a lance that bleeds. He follows Gornemant's advice and does not ask any questions. His host, stricken by a mysterious illness, retires. The next day, the castle is deserted.

As he is leaving, Perceval meets a young woman who is weeping for her lover, a knight. She tells him the story of the Fisher King and admonishes him for not asking his host about the procession of the grail. She says that she is his cousin and tells him that his mother has died.

Perceval is left with nothing to do, so he sets off again. He comes across the maiden he offended the day he left. She is condemned to a life of misery by her jealous lover, the Proud Knight of the Moor. Perceval confronts the Proud Knight and frees the young woman from his clutches.

King Arthur sets out to look for Perceval. The young man, who is contemplating drops of blood on the snow, fights the knights who call to him, but agrees to follow Gawain. At court, a very ugly maiden admonishes him for not speaking in the Fisher King's castle, because asking about the grail could have cured the king, who was the victim of a curse. Next, Guinganbresil arrives, accuses Gawain of killing his father and demands that he answer for his crime before the king of Escavalon.

Gawain

Gawain goes to see the king of Escavalon. On his way, he takes part in a tournament where he must defend his honour, then is unknowingly taken in by his enemy, the king himself. He falls in love with the king's sister. He is given an extra year to answer for his actions and accomplish his mission: bring back the bleeding lance.

Brief return to Perceval

Perceval has spent five years distinguishing himself, but has abandoned religion. He goes to confess to a hermit, who gives him advice and reveals that he is his uncle. He also tells him that the Fisher King is his cousin and that the grail, a chalice containing a host, keeps the king's father alive.

The continuation of Gawain's adventures

After a misfortune with Greoreas, Gawain goes to a dangerous enchanted castle. He frees the castle from the evil spells cast on it by sitting on the Wondrous Bed, earning the gratitude of the queen. He refuses to reveal his identity until seven days have passed.

Gawain meets Guiromelant, who tells him that the women in the castle are King Arthur's mother Ygerne and Gawain's own mother and sister. Guiromelant admits that he is in love with the sister, but that her brother Gawain is his worst enemy. Gawain then reveals his identity and the two men must duel.

THE CONTINUATIONS

EPISODE 1

King Arthur goes to Ygerne's castle. Gawain's sister sees to it that the duel is called off and marries her lover.

EPISODE 2

Perceval goes to the castle of Belrepeire, becomes wealthy, finds Blanchefor and promises to marry her in the future. He then leaves again to go on a quest.

EPISODES 3 AND 4

Perceval saves two knights, who have fallen victim to a magic column on a mountain, from madness. After a series of misfortunes, he decides to go to the mountain.

EPISODE 5

Perceval comes across a child perched in a tree who predicts that something will happen to him on the mountain; however, the knight escapes the evil spell. Merlin's daughter tells him the story of the magic column. Perceval goes to see the Fisher King, who explains all the mysteries he has encountered.

EPISODE 6

Perceval manages to destroy the Black Hand, an allegory of Satan, in a mysterious chapel. He continues on his way, but falls victim to some diabolical tricks. A lord comes to his aid.

EPISODE 7

Perceval learns that Belrepeire is under siege from Arides of Escavalon. He sets out to defend his lady and emerges victorious.

EPISODE 8

Perceval saves Gornemant of Gohort, whose castle is being attacked by forty knights who come back to life every time they are killed. This is because of an evil spell cast in order to eliminate Gornemant as punishment for dubbing Perceval, the future King of the Grail. Perceval marries Blancheflor.

EPISODE 9

Perceval meets Hector. After a duel, they are healed by the appearance of the grail. Perceval arrives at the castle of Pertinax, who kills all the knights who approach. Perceval cuts off his head and takes it to the Fisher King, thereby lifting the evil spell that has been placed on him. The Fisher King finds out that he is related to the young man and makes him his heir.

EPISODE 10

At King Arthur's court, the dangerous seat at the Round Table remains vacant: this is the seat for the King of the Grail. Perceval tries it, and in this way brings the six knights who died after trying to sit on it back to life.

EPISODES 11 AND 12

Perceval meets some monks who tell him the story of King Mordrain. Later on, he learns that the Fisher King is dead, so he must replace him. He reigns for seven years. After Blancheflor dies, he retires to a monastery to be a priest. When he dies, the grail and the bleeding lance disappear.

CHARACTER STUDY

PERCEVAL

We do not learn the name of Perceval of Wales, the hero of the first part of Chrétien's novel, until quite late on. He is the coddled son of a widowed lady, and it seems that the mention of his name coincides with him becoming an independent individual. At the start of the story, the reader does not know much about the character and, curiously, it seems that he does not know himself either: he "guessed" his name (p. 98), fails to recognise his cousin and is unaware of his origins. He is not described physically, but is simply presented as handsome and attractive. He appears to be very young, because he is referred to as a "boy", a term that was mainly used for children in the Middle Ages. As such, it seems that he can only really exist once he follows his destiny and becomes a knight.

When he begins his initiation into the world of the knights, Perceval is an extremely naïve and immature young man: even his remarkable courage and ambition seem to be governed by this naivety. He is incapable of discernment, since he follows all the advice he is given to the letter without thinking about the consequences of his actions. Furthermore, he does not seem to pay attention to his surroundings ("The young man did not care a chive for anything the king related", p. 31) and seems unfeeling. Even though he sees his mother falling as he is leaving, he does not go back to her, and does not appear to be sad when he finds out she has died. However, when he meets his cousin, he seems to become aware of his actions at the same time as his name. From that point on, the character develops into a wise knight who respects others. Chrétien therefore presents Perceval as a foolish young man who becomes a courtly knight thanks to a good education.

GAWAIN

Gawain is a respected knight with impressive ancestry, who belongs to the tradition of Arthurian tales. In Chrétien's writing, he embodies perfection: he is courageous, he is never defeated, and his actions are motivated by a keen sense of chivalry. Consequently, this handsome knight is the archetype of the kind of character that the naïve Perceval would like to be at the start of the novel. When Perceval is contemplating the drops of blood in the snow, the two men recognise one another. Perceval sees Gawain as his double, his knightly soulmate, and agrees to follow him. In this way, the author places the two men above the other knights.

However, their meeting seems to mark a turning point in the story and reverse their roles: Perceval embarks on a quest for the grail and has become a valiant knight at the king's court when Gawain must leave to restore his tarnished honour. Arthur's nephew, who had been irreproachable up to that point, loses some of his valour. He neglects his quest on multiple occasions (for example when he goes to see the king of Escavalon) and reveals himself to be proud: he hurries to Ygerne's castle because a boatman advises him against it. He is humiliated by Greoreas when he has to spur the war horse, leaving him in an undignified position for a knight. He is also untrustworthy: he promises loyalty and fidelity to two different women in the space of a few days.

We may wonder whether Chrétien's last novel marks Gawain's decline. This cannot be confirmed as the text was left unfinished, but many elements tarnish his status as a model knight, in favour of Perceval.

desire to be dubbed. Leaving his mother allows him to stop being foolish. The hero's lack of identity at the start of the novel is revealing: he is initially referred to by periphrases such as "the widowed lady's child" (p. 5), and does not become Perceval of Wales until p. 98. In this way, Chrétien shows that the character, who was initially insignificant and linked to his mother, only deserves his name after he has accomplished various feats. By becoming Perceval, the hero completes an important stage in his learning.

In the novel, the hero builds his identity through chivalry. He is given advice by three successive mentors who reveal to him the secrets of fulfilment: his mother, the gentleman Gornemant of Gohort and the hermit. These three characters offer him an increasingly sophisticated theoretical education. His training is completed as he deals with different events: he understands and acquires chivalric values as he takes part in battles and meets different people. The author highlights Perceval's development by emphasising his mistakes and the way he makes up for them afterwards. He initially offends the sleeping maiden, who refers to him as "a young Welsh fool, a clown, an oaf" (p. 25), but once he has become a valiant knight, he meets her again and saves her from the misery he has driven her to. The episode with the procession of the grail follows the same pattern: he makes the mistake of not asking a question, which results in misfortunes for the knights, but the continuations give him the opportunity to redeem himself and free the Fisher King from the evil spell. Chrétien, imitated by his successors, illustrates his hero's training with this story which comes full circle, making Perceval into a handsome and accomplished knight.

Perceval gradually discovers the important values of courage, chivalry and love. At the start of the story, he is inexperienced and clumsily familiarises himself with women through the sleeping maiden, before achieving the romantic ideal with Blancheflor. His introduction to love therefore goes hand in hand with his increasing knowledge of knighthood. His religious journey follows the same pattern: initially, his mother tells him to pray to God, but "every other prayer he knew, his mother had taught him to recite" (p. 8). He gains religious knowledge through his meeting with the hermit. We learn that, until this point, he has neglected his duties as a Christian, but his uncle puts him back on the right track by teaching him about the benefits of prayer and confession. After Chrétien's death, later writers went even further by having Perceval retire to a monastery after his beloved's death. At the same time as becoming a respected knight, Perceval also successfully masters love and religion.

CHIVALRY

Chivalry is one of the major themes of Chrétien's novel. In this story where there are women everywhere, knights are constantly torn between adventure and love. Conflict between the characters is mainly motivated by the need to help damsels in distress: they are trying to win the admiration of a lady based on the principles of courtly love, or *fin'amor* in Occitan. *Fin'amor* refers to a codified, deep and lasting love between two good people. Chrétien reproduces the rules of this art of love in his book through the relationship between Perceval and Blancheflor. The lady who is loved is noble and has a high social status. Her lover idealises her: "The Lord created her a wonder to steal men's hearts away as plunder, and never, since that time or later, has He bestowed a beauty greater on any girl to be her rival" (p. 53). The knight must demonstrate his devotion and carry out great feats to be worthy of the heart of his beloved: Perceval fights the enemies of Belrepeire and receives Blancheflor's love in return. He must also swear fidelity to her: we know that Perceval resists all the temptations he encounters throughout his adventures. *Fin'amor* therefore depicts an ideal love with the woman at its heart.

The notion of chivalry also extends to the social sphere. It defined all the rules for behaviour among the nobility in the Middle Ages. Goodness, courage, valour, a sense of honour and generosity were chivalrous qualities that noblemen should develop. As we have seen, Perceval gradually acquires them as he matures. Hospitality and respect for others are also intrinsic values in the world of chivalry.

The fact that chivalry is a constant presence throughout *Perceval, or, The Story of the Grail* shows that it belongs to the genre of the courtly romance which developed in the 11th and 12th centuries. The courtly romance, which was originally written in octosyllables (eight-syllable lines) or alexandrines (12-syllable lines), then in prose, recounts the fabulous, and above all chivalrous, adventures of knights.

A COMPLEX STRUCTURE

Perceval, or, The Story of the Grail has a complex structure and contains inconsistencies which may throw the reader off balance. The spatial and temporal references in the novel are disjointed: for example, the duration of events cannot correspond to the time indicated, Perceval contemplates the snow in June, and the five-year gap in his story is abrupt and does not fit well with the progression of events. There is no connection between the places the protagonists visit: we get the impression that the knights travel at random from one castle to the next, and King Arthur's court is particularly unstable (from Carduel to Carlion, via Orkney). Furthermore, some of the episodes have no outcome (we do not know the story of the extraordinary sword offered to Perceval, and Gawain and Guinganbresil's duel is put off until later) and the quest for the grail, from which the book takes its title, is quickly cast aside. The juxtaposition of the stories of Perceval and Gawain's adventures may even have led some critics to think that a copyist had tried to put two separate works together.

However, we can still detect unity in the novel. The switch to Gawain's adventures is not as abrupt as it may seem, since a link between the two heroes is established when Arthur's nephew asks about the young knight ("In God's name, sire, who is this knight...?", p. 112) and when he brings Perceval back to the court. In this way, Chrétien anticipates the shift from one knight to the other. The brief return to Perceval's journey illustrates the technique of intertwining plots, a feature of Arthurian tales.

Furthermore, there are many similarities between the adventures of Perceval and Gawain: they both have a connection to the bleeding lance, they both encounter ladies who have been insulted by being hit, and so on. Their journeys seem to be mirror images or inversely symmetrical: Perceval struggles to become a high-ranking and respected knight, whereas Gawain, who is already renowned, fights to restore his tarnished honour. Perceval loses his mother at the start of the story, while Gawain finds his at the end. The story of the adventures of the two knights therefore indicates the author's desire to place their destinies in parallel to one another and encourage the reader to compare them.

FURTHER REFLECTION

SOME QUESTIONS TO THINK ABOUT...

- What place does religion have in the novel?
- Perceval and Gawain's adventures introduce a fantastic element. How is this shown?
- Women are everywhere in the story. How do they embody both weakness and power?
- Perceval's battles have a symbolic function. What is it?
- In your opinion, what is Chrétien de Troyes' intention in establishing a parallel between Perceval and Gawain?
- *Perceval, or, The Story of the Grail* is one of the first chivalric romances. What are the characteristics of this genre? What are the signs that it is related to the genres of courtly poetry and the *chanson de geste*?
- In what way has *Perceval, or, The Story of the Grail* become a model in literature and the arts? Cite examples where it has served as inspiration.

*We want to hear from you!
Leave a comment on your online library
and share your favourite books on social media!*

FURTHER READING

REFERENCE EDITION

- De Troyes, C. (2011) *Perceval, or, The Story of the Grail*. Trans. Cline, R.H. Athens, Georgia: University of Georgia Press.

REFERENCE STUDIES

- Burgess, G.S. and Pratt, R. (2009) *The Arthur of the French: The Arthurian Legend in Medieval French and Occitan Literature (Arthurian Literature in the Middle Ages)*. Cardiff: University of Wales Press.
- Gray, M. (1992) *A Dictionary of Literary Terms (York Handbooks)*. London: Longman.
- Lacy, N.J. and Grimbert, J.T. eds. (2008) *A Companion to Chrétien de Troyes (Arthurian Studies)*. Woodbridge: D.S.Brewer.
- McGuinness, P. (2017) *French Poetry: From Medieval to Modern Times (Everyman's Library Pocket Poets)*. London: Everyman's Library.
- Schultz, J.A. (2006) *Courtly Love, the Love of Courtliness, and the History of Sexuality*. Chicago: University of Chicago Press.

ADAPTATION

- *Perceval le Gallois*. (1978) [Film]. Éric Rohmer. Dir. France: Les Films du Losange.

Rohmer chooses to remain close to the original text, but uses deliberately unrealistic scenery. Choruses are used to reproduce the descriptions between different scenes of action.

MORE FROM BRIGHTSUMMARIES.COM

- Reading guide – *Lancelot, or, The Knight of the Cart* by Chrétien de Troyes.
- Reading guide – *Yvain, the Knight of the Lion* by Chrétien de Troyes.

Bright ≡Summaries.com

More guides to rediscover your love of literature

www.brightsummaries.com

Although the editor makes every effort to verify the accuracy of the information published, BrightSummaries.com accepts no responsibility for the content of this book.

© BrightSummaries.com, 2016. All rights reserved.

www.brightsummaries.com

Ebook EAN: 9782806298638

Paperback EAN: 9782806298645

Legal Deposit: D/2017/12603/336

Cover: © Primento

Digital conception by Primento, the digital partner of publishers.

Made in the USA
Monee, IL
03 May 2026